Spencer Walpole

The British Fish Trade

Spencer Walpole

The British Fish Trade

ISBN/EAN: 9783743417885

Manufactured in Europe, USA, Canada, Australia, Japa

Cover: Foto ©Suzi / pixelio.de

Manufactured and distributed by brebook publishing software
(www.brebook.com)

Spencer Walpole

The British Fish Trade

International Fisheries Exhibition

LONDON, 1883

THE

BRITISH FISH TRADE

BY

HIS EXCELLENCY

SPENCER WALPOLE

LIEUT.-GOVERNOR OF THE ISLE OF MAN

LONDON

WILLIAM CLOWES AND SONS, LIMITED

INTERNATIONAL FISHERIES EXHIBITION

AND 13 CHARING CROSS, S.W.

1883

THE BRITISH FISH TRADE.

FEW things are more remarkable in modern politics than the care which is almost everywhere taken to illustrate, by statistics the science of government. In the United Kingdom elaborate arrangements are made with this object. Public officers are employed in enumerating the flocks and herds; in recording the crops which are sown; and in counting every bale of goods which is either imported into, or exported from, the country. The writer, who desires to procure statistical information on almost any subject connected with the growth, the health, the condition, or the industry of the people, is able to obtain it in an authoritative form, and in a convenient and cheap volume. The success which the "Statistical Abstracts" have achieved has induced their authors to extend their scope. The Statistical Abstract of the United Kingdom has been supplemented by statistical abstracts for the Colonies, for India, and for even foreign countries. A vast mass of information of almost immeasurable value has in this way been collected, and the student or the inquirer is able to obtain facts on almost every subject to which either his studies or his investigations may be directed.

Yet the politician or the student, who has had occasion to consult the excellent statistics which are published by the British Government, has probably noticed one remarkable omission from them. While on every other subject he finds information, which is usually full and which is seldom inexact, on one subject he fails to obtain any information whatever. The editor of the Statistical Abstract does not seem to be aware that a large number of persons in the British Islands are dependent on fishing for their livelihood ; that a considerable proportion of the food of the inhabitants of these islands consists of fish ; and that one of the most important trades of the kingdom is the trade in fish. The quantity of fish which is imported into these islands from abroad or which is exported from them is included in the statistical abstracts. But on the much greater questions which are connected with the fisheries— the employment which they afford, the capital which they attract, and the wealth which they produce—the Statistical Abstract is uniformly silent.

This silence arises from no fault of the editor of the Abstract. He gives no information on the subject of fisheries, because no full information is forthcoming which is worth publishing. The Fishery Board of Scotland, indeed, annually publishes elaborate and detailed accounts of the Scotch herring fishery. The Irish Inspectors of Fisheries also compile once a year some statistics—which, however, are admittedly imperfect—to illustrate the development, or rather the decay, of the Irish fisheries. But in England itself little information is afforded to the student who wishes to ascertain the condition of the English fisheries. The Inspectors of salmon fisheries are, indeed, required to report annually on the state of the English salmon fisheries. But the salmon fisheries of England and Wales stand in the same relation to the sea-fisheries of the country as Croydon to London, or Rutland to Yorkshire. The state of the more important fisheries has to be ascertained by reference to a number of more or less authoritative publications, and to be inferred, rather than proved, from a number of incidental circumstances. There are no means of ascertaining with any precision such simple facts as the number of boats employed, or the number of persons engaged, in the sea-fisheries of England and Wales.*

This absence of information naturally increases the difficulty of any writer who undertakes to describe the fish trade of the United Kingdom. Instead of moving on firm ground, he is perpetually fearing that the whole basis of his argument may give way as he advances. He is forced to adduce theories where he ought to state facts, and he has to prove elementary propositions which ought to be accepted as readily as axioms. The difficulty with which his task is thus surrounded is his fittest excuse for any imperfections on his part in completing it; and the best service, which he can perhaps hope to accomplish, is to induce the Government to supply some of the information, the publication of which would have made most of his own labours unnecessary.

And, in truth, if there be any subject on which statistical information is desirable, if there be any industry which

---

* A return is annually published, by the Registrar-General of Shipping and Seamen, of the number of boats, registered under the Sea Fisheries Act 1868, belonging to each port in the United Kingdom. But the return is imperfect for the following reason : "On the 23rd of October, 1877, an Order in Council was obtained by the Board of Trade, exempting from registration, &c., undecked boats, fishing or dredging on the coasts of England, Wales, and Scotland, and the Islands of Guernsey, Jersey, Sark, and Man, and not going outside the distance of three miles from low-water mark along the said coasts." Since the date of this order, which however never applied to Ireland, and from the operation of which Scotland was exempted in 1880, the Registry of fishing boats has become more and more imperfect.

deserves to be illustrated by figures stamped with the impress of authority, the fisheries and fishermen of this country deserve that recognition. The British Islands, from a fisherman's point of view, enjoy a singular advantage. There are no other waters in the globe so rich in food-producing fish as those of the North Atlantic Ocean ; and there is no portion of this great ocean so fishful as that part of it which surrounds these Islands. If, however, nature has placed the United Kingdom in a pre-eminently favourable position, the hardy inhabitants of its maritime counties have made the best use of nature's bounty. Their veins, still warm with the bold blood of their Saxon and Danish forefathers, the people of Eastern Britain especially have inherited a love for the sea. Few storms are so severe as to drive them from their occupation. Their well-found boats court dangers which other and larger vessels shun ; and, in the roughest as in the calmest weather, the dish of fish, which these bold men have risked lives and fortunes in catching, is procurable, if it consist of what the trade calls "offal," for a few pence ; if it be composed of what the trade calls "prime," for a few shillings in the London market.

Yet it must not be supposed that the inhabitants of all the maritime counties of Great Britain or of the United Kingdom furnish fishermen in equal proportions. It is Eastern Scotland and Eastern England which supplies the majority of British fishermen. Cornwall, Devonshire, and the Isle of Man are almost the only other parts of the kingdom which furnish a class of men who make fishing the sole occupation of their lives. In Ireland, indeed, a movement has, for years past, been in progress to develop the Irish fisheries. But the seas of Ireland are swept by Scotch, English, and Manx boats, and, though Irish craft are found fishing among them, the Irishmen rarely or never repair in their turn to the Scotch and English seas. In this respect they are not peculiar. The Highlanders and Islanders of Western Scotland, sprung from a common ancestry with the Irish, seldom leave their own lochs, or their own seas; the Welshman like the Irishman rarely, if ever, leaves his own neighbourhood; and Welsh boats are never seen in English seas. The Cornishman is perhaps the only example in the United Kingdom of a man sprung from a Celtic ancestry who follows his fish from sea to sea. In every other case, it may be suspected that the fishermen owe some of their skill and courage to the blood of the bold Saxon and Norse Sea Rovers, who, in the early days of English History, played their part in what the late Mr. Green has called the making of England.*

This circumstance is of essential importance. In the olden time fishing, conducted chiefly in the estuaries of rivers, or on the coasts of the sea, was a trade which required little skill, and perhaps little courage. Our forefathers while fishing did not venture far out to sea, but kept in close proximity to the shore, either in consequence of the frailty of their boats, or of what an early writer has called "the fearfulness" of their minds. Much of the fish which was served up on table was intercepted in passing out to sea with the ebb tide by the dams which any

---

* How far the Devonshire and Cornish people may owe their fishing propensities to the Conquest of South Western Britain by Egbert in 815 is perhaps doubtful. The Saxons, it is certain, did not succeed in rooting out the Celtic names which still distinguish this part of England. But the Saxon conquerors, in all probability, settled and fused with the Britons in Cornwall, while they only held a strategical position in Wales. No one, at any rate, can look at a Cornish fisherman at the present time, and think that he is descended from the same exclusively Celtic stock as the Welsh.

labourer, who had no more brains than Caliban in "The Tempest," was competent to build.* But the increasing demands of a populous country have altered this state of things. Fishermen are no longer able to wait for the fish to come to them, they go to the fish. Every year which passes sees the fishing conducted at greater distances from our coasts.

The best fish are frequently caught farthest from the land ; the most successful fishermen are consequently those who have the boldest hearts and the stoutest boats. They are those, therefore, who, other things being equal, have embarked most capital in their trade. But the man who has invested his fortune in any business cannot afford to let his stock lie idle. He must, if he hope to profit from his investment, constantly use it. The fisherman, however, who would fish throughout the year to advantage, must be prepared to lead a nomad life. Fish are caught in one part of the ocean in one month, and in another in another. The fishermen who follow the fish, or, in stricter phrase, go to those seas where the fish are found, will always beat the fishermen who fish their own seas, and, when fishing is no longer profitable there, eke out a scanty livelihood with other work. In the case of the latter, their capital lies idle while the capital of their rivals is employed, and they themselves are destitute of the experience which their rivals acquire. The fishermen of

---

* The passage in " The Tempest " is curious. Caliban sings :
"No more dams I'll make for fish ;
Nor fetch in firing
At requiring,
Nor scrape trenchering, nor wash dish."
The duties with which Shakespeare associates Caliban are of a menial character requiring no skill ; and the dam was evidently a temporary and not a permanent structure.

the east coast of Britain, the Manxmen, and the Cornish-men follow the fish from coast to coast, and, in consequence, the whole fishing trade of the country is passing into their hands.

It may, perhaps, be convenient, before describing the fisheries themselves, to state approximately the employment which they afford. In England and Wales there are probably about 15,000 fishing boats, affording permanent employment to 28,000, and temporary employment to 14,000 persons. The English statistics are, however, notoriously imperfect, and no great reliance can be placed on them. In Scotland there were, in 1881, according to the Report of the Scotch Fishery Board, 14,809 boats employing 48,121 persons ; in Ireland the Irish inspectors state that there were in the same year 6458 vessels employing 24,528 men and boys ; but they add that only 1844 of these boats and 7534 of these persons were exclusively engaged in fishing. In the Isle of Man some 450 boats gave almost continuous employment to 2872 fishermen ; while in the Channel Islands some 300 boats sustained about 1000 fishermen. In the British Islands, therefore, some 37,000 boats give constant or occasional employment to 118,000 fishermen.

It will at once be seen from these figures that the fishing population is distributed unevenly through the different branches of the Empire. England and Wales has one fisherman for about every 600 of its people ; Ireland has one fisherman for every 200 of its inhabitants ; Scotland has one fisherman for every 75 ; and the Isle of Man has one fisherman for every 19 of its population. But the statistics would look very different if they were applied to particular localities. Of the 42,000 fishermen of England and Wales, nearly one-third, or 13,000, sail from the four great ports of the Eastern counties—Grimsby, Hull, Yar-

mouth, and Lowestoft—nearly one-sixth, or 6,000, sail from
the great Cornish and Devonshire ports—Penzance, Fal-
mouth, Fowey, Plymouth, and Dartmouth. These nine
ports, therefore, supply nearly one-half of all the fishermen
of England and Wales. The whole coast line of Wales
does not support so many fishermen as the single town
of Lowestoft, or the Isle of Man.

It must not be supposed that the 118,000 fishermen of
the British Islands are the only persons dependent on
fishing. The Scotch Commissioners estimate that, while
there are 48,000 fishermen in Scotland, there are 48,000
other persons (curers, coopers, &c.) dependent on the
fisheries. It is unlikely that a similar proportion is to be
found in other portions of the United Kingdom. The
Scotch trade, as will hereafter be shown, is essentially a
trade in cured fish ; the English, Irish, and Manx trade is
chiefly a trade in fresh fish. It does not require any
elaborate argument to show that a trade in cured fish must
necessarily employ more persons than a trade in fresh fish.
Perhaps it may be safe to assume that, while every fisherman afloat in Scotland finds employment for one · other
person on shore, every two fishermen in the rest of the
British Islands finds work for one other person. In that
case the 48,000 fishermen of Scotland give work to 48,000
other persons ; and the 70,000 other fishermen in the British
Islands afford employment to 35,000 other persons. And
thus the grand total may be reached, that 201,000, or say
200,000, people are dependent on the fisheries of the British
Islands for their livelihood.

It is probably even more difficult to ascertain exactly the
amount of capital embarked in the fisheries than to estimate the extent of work which they afford. But, in this
respect, help may again be derived from the returns of

the Scotch Commissioners. They estimate the total value of the boats and gear of the Scotch fishermen at £1,400,000. It is certain that the value of each boat in Ireland is not greater than the value of each boat in Scotland. Placing it at about the same sum the capital employed in the Irish sea fisheries may perhaps be computed at £600,000. The value of the English boats is much greater than the value of the Scotch or of the Irish boats. In Ireland and Scotland most of the boats are engaged in drift fishing; and a first-class drift boat, with herring gear complete, is worth about £550. But in England a large proportion of the boats is engaged either in trawling or in line fishing; and a first-class trawler, ready for sea, cannot cost less than £1,000 or £1,200; while a cod-smack, fitted for line fishing, is worth £1,500. It is certain, therefore, that the average value of the 15,000 English boats is much greater than the average value of the 15,000 Scotch boats. Placing it at twice the sum, the capital embarked in the English fisheries must amount to £2,800,000. The capital embarked in the Manx fisheries is about £240,000; and a gross capital of about £5,000,000 is, therefore, probably employed in the fisheries of the British Islands.

Thus then, to summarise the conclusions which have been already stated, some 200,000 persons are probably employed in the fisheries of the British Islands; and some £5,000,000 of capital are embarked in these industries. These figures enable a rough estimate to be formed of the produce of the fisheries. If it be assumed that every person employed in fishing earns only £40 a year, and that only 10 per cent. is required to pay the interest on, and to replace, the capital engaged, the sea fisheries of the British Islands must yield a gross sum of £8,500,000 annually. If to this sum be added a further £800,000, the estimated produce of the Scotch, Irish, and English salmon fisheries, it will be seen that the gross value of the British fisheries must be fixed at some £9,300,000, or say from £9,000,000 to £10,000,000 a year. It will be shown later on that other figures, derived from independent sources, go a long way towards confirming the accuracy of this estimate.

The fish which are caught in the British seas may be divided, for the purposes of this argument, into two classes : 1. Bottom fish, or fish which live at or near the bottom of the sea. 2. Floating fish, or fish which swim at or near the surface of the water. The former class comprises (*a*) flat fish, such as turbot, brill, halibut, sole, plaice, and others ; and (*b*) round fish, as they are called in contradistinction to flat fish, such as cod, haddock, and ling. The most important fish in the latter class are the *clupeidæ* (herrings, pilchards, sprats) and mackerel. It will be readily understood that fish which live at or near the bottom of the sea must be caught by engines different from those employed for the capture of fish swimming at or near the surface of the water. As a matter of fact the fish in the first class are caught mainly either by the trawl-net or by lines ; while fish in the latter class are taken chiefly in drift-nets and seine nets. It may, perhaps, be desirable, before proceeding further with the narrative, to describe very briefly these several modes of fishing.

The hook and line, which is still extensively used, is one of the most ancient modes of fishing in the world. " Canst thou draw out Leviathan with a hook ? " so commences a well-known passage in Job ; while in Homer men fish with hooks, both in the Odyssey and in the Iliad, though in both poems the hooks are made of horn. Line fishing, however, as it is now practised differs widely from the art which the ancients used. The Grimsby smacks employed in this trade are the largest and most costly vessels employed in fishing. The "fleet" of lines which each boat places at the bottom of the sea is about seven or eight miles long ; and each "fleet" contains from about 4000 to 5000 hooks. It will be readily understood that the mere task of baiting these hooks involves an enormous amount of labour ; and that the work of supplying bait forms of itself a considerable industry. The growing scarcity of mussels, which form the best and most convenient bait, and the irksome toil inseparable from baiting the long lines, are perhaps slowly tending to supersede this mode of fishing with trawling. A trawl net is a stout purse-like net, with a wide mouth at one end, tapering almost to a point at the other end. The mouth of the net is kept open by the upper portion of it being attached to a heavy beam of wood, which is supported at either end by two heavy iron sledge-like contrivances. The lower portion of the net lies at the bottom of the sea. The beam of the largest trawl nets is 50 feet in length ; and the great fish markets of the kingdom are dependent for a large portion of their supplies of fish on the operations of the trawlers. The fish caught in the trawl are usually dying or dead when they are drawn on to the deck of the vessel. The fish caught by the lines, on the contrary, are generally alive. The line smacks, therefore, are usually fitted with wells or chambers into which the sea water is admitted, and the fish are brought in these wells alive to land. There, many of the cod are kept either in chests or cases anchored in the sea ; or more simply, though more cruelly, are tied together by the tails, and kept in salt water till they are required for the market. Then they are drawn up, killed, and sold as live cod— killed, as the technical phrase runs, "to save their lives."

Such are the chief modes by which bottom fish are caught. Surface fish, it has already been stated, are mostly taken either by the seine or the drift net. The seine-net— a net by which the fish are encompassed, and either drawn up on to the shore, or "tucked" into the boat in mid ocean—is probably the oldest movable net used by man. It is largely employed by the Americans in mackerel fishing; but, except in the pilchard fishery of Cornwall, in the herring fishery of south-western Scotland, and in the salmon fishery, it is not extensively employed in this country. The drift net—a net which floats in the passage of the fish, and in which the fish are caught by enmeshing themselves—is the engine by which the herrings and mackerel are chiefly taken. A first-class boat, fishing for herrings, will carry a drift net or fleet of drift nets nearly two miles long. It is computed that the Scotch herring nets alone would stretch four times across the Atlantic from Liverpool to New York.

Drift nets were originally made of hemp; in Ireland and the Isle of Man they were till lately made of flax; they are now almost universally made of cotton. The greater lightness of the cotton has enabled the fishermen to extend the length of the net, and, in consequence, the efficiency of the engine. But the labour of hauling in even a cotton net two miles long is enormous; and to facilitate the work, many of the best boats have of late years been provided with small auxiliary steam engines. It seems possible that, when these engines are brought into more general use, it will be found convenient to supplement the boats with an auxiliary screw; and thus the whole fishing trade may, in consequence, be ultimately carried on, under certain conditions, by steam vessels. This revolution, how-ever, is not yet accomplished. Excepting a few steam trawlers, fishing vessels are in all parts of the kingdom dependent on their sails, and, in consequence, great attention has been paid to the rig of the vessels.

There are probably few people, even among those who are best acquainted with the fisheries, who are at all aware of the great alteration which is taking place in this respect. Originally the boats used as trawlers were usually cutter-rigged ; the boats used for drift fishing were lugger-rigged. An example of the old rig of trawlers may still be found in Cornwall and in the south of England ; and the Scotch and east of England drift boats are still usually rigged as luggers. But experience is gradually leading to the supercession of both these rigs. As the trawlers increase in size, the large mainsail of the cutter is found too heavy for the men to work, and in consequence the large trawlers on the east coast have been built with a small mizen mast ; the size of the mainsail is thereby reduced, and a small manageable mizen added. A similar alteration is being gradually made in the rig of the drift-boats. The old lug-sail has to be lowered on each tack and re-hoisted. Such an operation in large boats naturally involves a great deal of labour. The lugger, therefore, is being superseded by the dandy-rigged vessel ; and the dandy promises to be the rig which will ultimately be adopted by all classes of fishing-boats.*

* Fishermen use a "dandy" rigged boat, a "dandy" wink, and in hand-line fishing a "dandy" line. Mr. Holdsworth, in his book on deep-sea fishing, says that the "dandy" wink is the small wink or windlass astern of the boat used for hauling in the trawl (p. 67, note). The name "dandy" line, he writes in another passage, is not very intelligible . . . . The manner in which the line is worked by moving it gently up and down points strongly, however, to "dandle," as the real name (p. 154). But, if his interpretation be right in one case, why should it not apply to all three ? The dandy mast would then be the

Any change of rigging, which relieves the work of the fishermen, necessarily enables them to prosecute their calling with more profit, since it allows them to work their boat with a smaller crew. The crews which fishing-boats carry depend on the trade in which they are engaged. A first-class trawler will carry three, or in some cases four, men and a boy; a first-class drift boat requires seven men and a boy;* while a large Grimsby smack will carry nine to eleven hands. In most parts of the British Islands the fishermen have an interest in the proceeds of the fishery. The owner of the boat, the owner of the net, and the fisherman, all taking a certain proportion of the profits. In most parts of the British Islands, again, the lads who are employed in the boats are the near relatives of the fishermen engaged. But on the east coast of England, and at Hull and Grimsby in particular, a different system has arisen, and large numbers of lads, strangers to the fishermen and unacquainted with the sea, are apprenticed to the fishing trade. As the condition of these apprentices has attracted a good deal of attention of late years, it may be desirable to add a few words upon it.

It is not difficult to determine the reasons which have induced the boat-owners of Hull and Grimsby to engage apprentices. The large smacks which are fitted for line fishing require the services of many hands; but they only need comparatively inexperienced labour. Almost any boy can be trusted to bait a hook; to haul in a line; or to take a fish off a hook. More unskilled labour is thus required

---

short or small mizen mast; the dandy wink the small windlass; and the dandy line the small hand-line in contradistinction to the long line.

* This is the crew carried in Scotland and the Isle of Man. A still larger crew is carried by the Yarmouth boats.

in this branch of fishing than in any other. It so happens that Grimsby is situated at a convenient distance from the metropolis, where the Guardians of the Poor have always a large number of boys whom they are anxious to dispose of. A philanthropist might readily conclude that nothing could, under such circumstances, be better than to apprentice the boy to the healthy life of a fisherman. Yet philanthropy, unluckily, makes terrible mistakes when it acts without sufficient knowledge and without adequate inquiry. It is not every boy who has either the strength or the courage which fits him for the hard sea-faring life of a fisherman. It is not every master of a vessel who has the patience or the heart to make allowances for the short-comings of a timid, weak lad. In consequence, a system which was intended to work for good, has undoubtedly led to much evil. Some impatient masters have cruelly treated their boys, other boys have tried to escape the fate of their comrades by absconding from the boats and breaking their indentures. The magistrates have been compelled to punish the lads who have broken their engagement, while, in strict justice, the punishment ought perhaps to have fallen on the ill-advised people who sent them into an unsuitable calling. In 1875 no less than 375 apprentices—or on an average, rather more than one apprentice each day—were committed to the County Prison in Lincolnshire, or the Borough Prison in Hull. Some cases of unusual cruelty have since attracted the attention of the public to the position of these poor friendless boys, and the Board of Trade has appointed a committee to enquire into the subject. It may be hoped that the report which has thus been obtained may be the means of alleviating the lot of these lads. But the true method of terminating the abuses which have occurred, is to take care that the lads who go to sea shall be, as far as possible, the sons or relatives of the fishermen who go with them, or shall at any rate have parents or guardians living at the ports. The lot of a lad, far from home, far from friends, who is forced to spend much of his life on board a fishing-boat far from land, must be uncertain, unless it is protected by some such influences.*

The trawlers, the line smacks, and the drift-boats, all frequently fish the same waters. Trawlers, indeed, can only work in those parts of the sea where the bottom is soft and smooth. The trawl easily gets caught by a rocky bottom, and the operations of the trawler are stopped or his gear lost. But, with this exception, trawlers and drift-boats commonly fish the same waters. It will be readily understood that different classes of fishermen, using different modes of fishing and working in the same places, occasionally come into collision. A drift-boat, drifting with two miles of net in front of it is almost helpless, and a trawler coming across the net may break through it and carry away a portion of it. The law, indeed, has provided against losses of this character ; it has forbidden the trawlers to come within three miles of the drift-boat. But,

---

* The following are the chief recommendations made by the Committee.

(*a*) No lad under the age of 16 should be permitted to serve on board a vessel exceeding 20 tons net register tonnage, except under a written agreement, or an indenture of apprenticeship, to which the Mercantile Marine Superintendent or the Board of Trade Officer of the district must be a party, with the power to act as the guardian and protector of the lad.

(*b*) No lad to be indentured before he has reached the age of 13, or for a longer period than seven years.

(*c*) A month's trial of the sea life to be allowed to a lad before his indentures are made absolutely binding.

(*d*) The master, in every case, to be held responsible for the lodging and food of the lad on shore as well as at sea.

when large fleets of trawlers and drift vessels, or "drivers" (as they are called), are fishing on the same ground at the same time, as they do for instance in Mount's Bay, it is no easy matter for a fisherman to carry out the law ; and the difficulty is increased from the fact that drift-fishing is carried on solely at night.*

Provision, indeed, has been made against these collisions, the different classes of boats being required to carry distinctive lights. A trawler is required to carry one white light on its mast-head. A driver is directed by the Sea Fisheries Act, 1867, to carry two lights, one above another, three feet apart. So far the directions are plain enough.

---

* In the text allusion has only been made to accidental collision. A good deal of angry feeling has, however, lately been provoked by the discovery that some foreign trawlers were in the habit of carrying a sharp instrument which they dragged behind them for the purpose of cutting through the warp or rope of any drift-net which fouled the trawl. The instrument, which received the expressive nickname of a devil, caused great mischief to the nets of the drift fishermen. Their loud remonstrances induced the Government to propose the appointment of an International Convention to enquire into the matter. The Convention, which was attended by representatives from Great Britain, Belgium, Denmark, France, Germany, and the Netherlands, met at the Hague in 1882. It agreed on the following articles :

" The use of any instrument or engine which serves only to cut or destroy nets is forbidden. The presence of any such engine on board a boat is also forbidden. The high contracting parties engage to take the necessary measures for preventing the embarkation of such engines on board fishing-boats.

" The high contracting parties engage to propose to their respective legislatures, the necessary measures for ensuring the execution of the present convention, and particularly for the punishment by either fine or imprisonment, or by both, of persons who may contravene the provisions."

The convention still awaits ratification ; but it is expected that it will before long be ratified and brought into effective operation by laws being passed in the countries which were parties to it.

C

Unluckily the person who drew them does not seem to have observed that the Merchant Shipping Act, 1862, contained contrary orders. This act declared that all fishing-boats, when attached to their nets and stationary, should carry one white light, and that this light, and no other, should be carried. These conflicting instructions involved the drift fishermen in a singular dilemma. If they obeyed the rules in the Merchant Shipping Act, they necessarily disobeyed the Sea Fisheries Act. They could not, on the other hand, observe the Sea Fisheries Act without contravening the Merchant Shipping Act. After some years Parliament came to their assistance, and directed them to follow the orders of the Merchant Shipping Act. But this decision led to a fresh inconvenience. It forced drift-nets and trawlers to carry the same lights, and consequently made it impossible for the trawlers to distinguish the drivers. The inconvenience was so great that the Government undertook to effect a remedy. It placed itself in communication with other countries, and endeavoured to arrange a new system of lighting to which the fishermen of all nations should be bound to conform. After years of negotiation, a new arrangement was made under which drift-net fishermen were required to carry two red lights, one above the other ; and trawlers were bound to carry a red and green light, one above the other. But the new regulations proved almost as unacceptable to the trade as the law which they had been framed to supersede. Neither red nor green lights can be seen at anything like the distance at which white lights of equal power are visible ; and it is probably impossible to devise a red light which it will be practicable for a fisherman to use, and a fishing-boat to carry, and which will be visible for three miles. This objection was raised so loudly that the Government was forced to suspend the operation of the new rule before it ever came into force. Since that time various proposals have been made for obviating the difficulty. But nothing has yet come of these proposals ; and the whole subject still remains in an unsettled state.

The development of the fishery is constantly increasing the difficulty of devising adequate means for keeping the trawlers and drift-nets apart. But there is one portion of the British Islands where collisions of this character rarely occur. Except in the Frith of Forth and on the Ayrshire coast, there is little or no trawling in Scotland ; * and the chief portion of the Scotch fishery is conducted by drift-nets and line fishermen. This circumstance, however, does not constitute the whole distinction between Scotland and the rest of the United Kingdom. In England, with few important exceptions, the bulk of the fish caught are caught for the fresh market and for the home trade ; in Scotland most of the fish are caught for the foreign market and are cured. The foreign trade in fish is of such importance that it may be desirable to describe it in some detail before proceeding to a review of the still more valuable home trade.

And, in the first place, it may surprise some people to learn that the import trade in fish is as important, and growing at least as rapidly, as the export trade. In 1842, forty-one years ago, 137,000 cwt. of fish were imported into the United Kingdom ; in 1882, 862,000 cwt., worth £1,659,000, were so imported. In 1842, on the other hand,

---

* In Scotland the word "trawl" is in common use. But the trawl of Scotland is not the beam-trawl of England, but the scine-net. It may be added that in the United States the trawl is the long line. There seems to be something peculiarly irritating to fishermen in the name of trawl. Scotch fishermen denounce the seine-net as " a trawl : " English fishermen denounce the beam-trawl ; and American fishermen object to the long lines which they call trawls.

162,000 barrels of herrings and fish of other sorts, worth £82,000, were exported ; in 1882, 920,000 barrels of herrings, worth £1,383,000, and fish of other kinds, worth £440,000, were sent abroad. The import trade has increased rather more, the export trade rather less, than sixfold in the forty years. The export trade is divided into four branches. The first and most important is the trade in Scotch herrings ; the second is the trade in cured cod and ling ; the third is the trade in Cornish pilchards ; the fourth is the trade in fresh fish with Paris and other Continental towns. The causes which produce trade are curious ; the demands which create it difficult of explanation. The earliest and most valuable Scotch herrings are sold to the upper classes in Northern and Eastern Europe ; the bulk of the Scotch herrings are consumed in the Protestant States of Germany ; Cornish pilchards find their principal market in Italy ; while the cod and ling, which are caught chiefly in the Shetland Islands and Northern Scotland, are sold in Spain. It is not, at first sight, clear why the German should prefer a herring to a pilchard, and an Italian the pilchard to a herring. But the Italian is usually a Roman Catholic ; the Roman Catholics buy fish as food, and the Italian, therefore, purchases a rich oily fish like the pilchard. The higher classes in Spain buy cod for the same reasons which make the salt cod of Newfoundland the usual dish in English households on the first and last day of Lent. The German Protestant, on the contrary, eats his herrings, not as his chief food, but as a relish. He likes his herrings, as he likes his hams, cured by salt, but uncooked by fire.

It is said in Northern Scotland that the trade between Spain and the Shetland Isles in dried fish has existed since the reign of Elizabeth. Some vessels of the great Armada were wrecked in the Shetlands; the crews were forced to remain there for many months, and, during their residence, they formed relations with the inhabitants which, after an interval of nearly three centuries, are still maintained by their descendants. About 4,000,000 cod and ling * are annually caught by Scotch fishermen; the catch produces about 150,000 cwt. of cured fish, and rather more than half. of the whole are exported from Scotland.

It is impossible to give any exact statistics of the produce of the pilchard fishery, because there is a large and increasing consumption of fresh pilchards in Cornwall and the adjoining counties. But a private firm has, for many years, published statistics of the export trade in this fish, which may be relied on with confidence. From these accounts it is evident that the pilchard fishery is one of the most uncertain of the harvests of the sea. Since 1869 the export trade has varied from rather more than 6,000 hogsheads in 1869 to nearly 46,000 hogsheads in 1870. But the average export trade of pilchards may probably be placed at about 12,000 hogsheads a year, the average value at about £3 a hogshead.

The curing of pilchards is not carried on with much care. The fish are piled on the stone floors of the curing-houses in masses five or six feet high, each layer of fish being covered with salt. The "bulk," as it is termed, is left thus piled up for a month. During this period the weight of the mass forces the oil out of the fish, and this

---

* The cod fishery of Scotland is probably capable of development. It is insignificant compared with the Norwegian cod fishery. " I was informed by Mr. Smidt, the Secretary to the Society for the Propagation of the Norwegian Fisheries, that the coast of Norway, from the Lofoten Islands (latitude 68° N.) to Finmark (latitude 71° N.), annually produces 50,000,000 cod fish, but the production in 1877 amounted to 70,000,000 cod " (20th Ann. Rep. Insp. Salmon Fisheries, p. 22.)

oil is run into cisterns and is used by the poor of Cornwall for lighting purposes. At the end of the month the fish are taken from the bulk and packed in hogsheads. As each hogshead contains about 2,500 fish, and is worth, according to the season, from about £2 to about £4, five to ten cured pilchards are sold for one penny. It is, perhaps, doubtful whether the same amount of nutritious animal food is procurable at as low a price in any other part of Europe.

It must, however, be admitted that, if pilchards cured in Cornwall form a cheap article of food, very little care is exercised by the curer. Far different is the course pursued with Scotch herrings. The Scotch herring fishery has been a favourite object of protective legislation. Sir Robert Peel, in the great debates on free trade, once declared that every one was in favour of free trade until his own interests were affected : he had "a Scotch correspondent who was a good free trader in everything except herrings." Many Scotchmen of the present day, who would resent the allegation that they were Protectionists as an insult, are still, in their hearts, of the same opinion as Sir Robert Peel's correspondent, and think that free trade is inapplicable to herrings. Yet the Scotch herring fishery is a standing example of the wisdom of free trade ; and it is probable that the remnant of protection which still clings to it is actually more harmful than beneficial to the fishermen.

The Scotch herring fishery has had a history of about 120 years. In the first half of the last century, Young, in a passage in the " Night Thoughts," which has frequently been quoted, declared that the British looked on

" Shamefully passive, while Batavia's fleet
    Defrauds us of the glittering finny swarms,
    That heave our firths, and crowd upon our shores."

The complaint which was thus raised by Young was echoed in other quarters ; and in 1750 a company was formed with a nominal capital of £500,000 for managing the fishery. But the company was not left dependent on its own exertions. Parliament offered a bounty of 30s. a ton on all decked vessels fitted out for the fishery, and Frederick, Prince of Wales, the father of George III., became the patron of the company. But neither the patronage of the Court nor the bounty of Parliament saved the enterprise from failure. In 1757 the company was forced to ask for higher bounties, and, in the thirty years ending in 1782, Parliament actually spent more than £300,000 in developing a fishery which, notwithstanding this expenditure, was with difficulty supported. In 1786 a new society, which still exists, was formed for the extension of the fishery. The society purchased estates in Mull, in Skye, on the west coast of Ross-shire, and subsequently at Wick on the east coast of Caithness, and built on them fishermen's houses. But it achieved only a doubtful success. It has long since ceased to take any direct part in the fishery, though it still draws from its property an income which is heavily burdened. It is very doubtful whether it has, in any way whatever, effected the object of its promoters.*

The system of bounties, which was originally thought indispensable for the prosperity of the fishery, continued to exist for more than fifty years after its institution. Bounties were granted, in the first instance, on every ton of shipping

* It is an instructive circumstance that the Germans, this century, have undergone the same experience which disappointed our forefathers last century. A company has been formed by some patriotic Germans to promote the German herring fishery. It has been supported by loans free from interest, and by heavy protective duties. Yet " neither help at home nor protection against the foreigner enables the company to flourish."—Inspector's 20th Ann. Rep., p. 29.

employed in the fishery. The result was obvious. As
Adam Smith put it in the "Wealth of Nations," vessels
were fitted out to catch the bounty, and not to catch the
fish. This evident result induced a Protectionist Parliament
to propound a fresh remedy. In addition to the bounties
on the tonnage of the vessels, a bounty of 2s., which was
subsequently raised to 4s., was paid on every barrel of
herrings cured. There is no doubt that under this system
the fishery was rapidly developed. The number of herrings
cured rose from about 90,000 barrels in 1809 to more than
350,000 barrels in 1828, when the bounty was abolished.
But it is not clear whether the vast increase in the trade
was due to the existence of the bounty. During the nine-
teen years which succeeded the abolition of the bounty the
trade continued to increase at an almost equal rate, and
560,000 barrels of herrings were cured in 1847, 640,000
barrels in 1848, and 770,000 barrels in 1849.

Bewildered, perhaps, at the rapid increase of a trade
which, in the first instance, had seemed to require so much
fostering protection, many people imagined that the increase
of the fishery must produce its own ruin, and that a fish
which was being caught in season and out of season would
sooner or later be exterminated. Influenced by such
arguments as these, Parliament in 1851 adopted a new
policy, and initiated a system of restrictive legislation.
These restrictive measures retarded the development of the
fishery, and, at the close of the seventeen years during
which they lasted, the average quantity of herrings cured
was no larger than it had been at the beginning. In 1867,
in accordance with the wise recommendation of a special
commission, restrictive legislation was repealed. The
fishery, in consequence, increased ; and in 1874, for the first
time in its history, upwards of 1,000,000 barrels of herrings

were cured. Then, however, a decrease to 942,000 barrels
in 1875, and to 598,000 barrels in 1876, created a fresh
alarm. A new Commission was appointed to investigate the
allegation that the fishery was being over fished. The Commission thought the decrease was due to accidental causes,
and declined to recommend a return to protective measures.
Their opinion has been justified by the result. In the five
succeeding years the fishery yielded on an average 1,035,000
barrels a year. In 1880 no less than 1,473,000 barrels of
herrings were cured in Scotland.

This rapid increase is the more remarkable because the
great majority of the herrings cured have always been
cured for export, and the course of the export trade has
entirely changed. During the first third of the present
century most of the herrings were exported either to the
West Indies or to Ireland. The slave-owners of the West
Indies found Scotch herrings a cheap food for their slaves,
and bought large quantities of them annually. But the trade
was actually destroyed by the abolition of slavery, and the
export of herrings, to "places out of Europe," which had
always exceeded 50,000 barrels, and which occasionally
was more than 80,000 barrels, dwindled away to nothing.
Ireland, however, still continued to purchase large quantities of herrings till after the famine of 1847. The poverty
of the people in the first instance, and the rapid decrease of
the population afterwards, terminated the Irish demand;
and Ireland, instead of taking 100,000, or even 180,000
barrels of herrings a year, now only purchases about 20,000
barrels annually.

Thus the two main markets, which had stimulated the
growth of the Scotch herring fishery during the first half
of the present century, were cut off from the exporter, and,
if no new demand had arisen, the trade must have perished.

At the time, however, at which the Irish and West Indian markets were closed, a variety of circumstances stimulated the Continental demand for Scotch herrings. The trade with the Continent commenced in the closing year of the great war. But up to 1843 the Continent never purchased 100,000 barrels of Scotch herrings. Since that time the Continental trade has been rapidly developed. The measures of Sir Robert Peel had probably, indirectly, the effect of enabling Germans and Russians to increase their purchases, while the reduction and the ultimate repeal of the timber duties lessened the cost of the barrels in which the herrings were packed. The Continent purchased upwards of 250,000 barrels of herrings in 1850, upwards of 290,000 barrels in 1860, 486,000 barrels in 1870, and 976,000 barrels in 1880. The whole of this vast increase, it should be recollected, has taken place during a period in which bounties have ceased, and in which trade, so far as this country is concerned, has been free.

It must not be supposed that this great trade in fish has risen without difficulty or without competition. On the contrary, the Germans have for some years placed heavy import duties on cured herrings with the express intention of protecting their own fishermen. But protection has proved absolutely powerless to develop the fisheries of Germany; and the German fishing fleet, though it is fostered by the patronage of the wealthy and protected by the import duties of the Legislature, lies idle in Emden, while the German markets are supplied by Norwegian, Dutch, and British fishermen. The competition of Norway and Holland has, in fact, proved much more formidable than the import duties of the German Legislature, and, if Britain should ever lose the trade, the loss will apparently be due to the competition of these nations and not to the protective duties of Germany. The increased attention, which both Dutch and Norwegian fishermen are paying to the cure, is being rewarded by a constantly increasing sale of Dutch and Norwegian herrings in German markets.*

In the past all three nations have taken exceptional measures to secure the sale of their own fish. The Dutch, Norwegian, and British Governments have been in the habit of branding the barrels in which the herrings are packed ; and the brand has been taken as a guarantee both of the quantity as well as of the quality of the fish. In Scotland the brand is a survival of the bounty system. The bounty was paid on each barrel of herrings branded, and the brand was retained after the bounty had been abolished.

A system, which has no example in any other industry, which is a mere survival of a policy of protection, and which is opposed to all the maxims which regulate modern legislation, has naturally been the subject of attack. In 1848 the Treasury instructed one of the ablest members of the Civil Service—the late Sir John Lefevre—to enquire into the matter. Sir John naturally reported that "the system of authenticating the quality of goods by the agency of a Government officer is objectionable in prin-

* The figures will be found in the Appendix to the Report of the Select Committee on the Scotch Herring Brand. It is there stated, on the authority of a Report published in 1857, that the quantity of herrings imported from Great Britain into the ports of Stettin, Königsberg, Hamburg, Dantzic, and Harburg, increased from 100,297 barrels in 1848 to 318,263 barrels in 1855 ; whilst the Dutch imports into the same places declined from 5,019 to 1,300 barrels, and the Norwegian from 194,862 to 122,423 barrels. In 1879, however, Norway sold to Germany 630,127 barrels ; Scotland 545,993 barrels, and Holland 98,026 barrels. It is plain, if these figures are reliable, that the Dutch and Norwegian trades are increasing more rapidly than the Scotch trade.

ciple ;" but he hesitated to risk the possible "derangement and contraction" of the foreign trade, which he thought might result from its abandonment. He took the middle course, therefore, of suggesting that a fee should be charged for the brand, and that the enterprising curer should be encouraged, by the prospect of saving his fee, to rely on his own brand instead of that of the Government. Nothing came of the report till 1855, when the Treasury decided on abolishing the brand. The remonstrances, however, which the decision excited in Scotland induced it, instead of abolishing the brand, to appoint a new Commission to enquire into it. The new Commissioners spoke with an uncertain sound. One of them recommended the termination of the system ; two of them adopted Sir John Lefevre's compromise, and proposed that the brand should be retained, but that a fee should be charged for it. The Treasury adopted the advice of the majority of the Commissioners, the brand was saved, and the fee was imposed.

This arrangement has not, however, had the effect of terminating the controversy. In 1866 an able Commission, the ablest Commission to which the subject of fisheries has ever been referred, condemned the brand ;* in 1870, however, a new Commission appointed by the Treasury declined "to undertake the responsibility of advising" its discontinuance. Finally in 1881, a Select Committee of the House of Commons recommended its retention.

These various reports and conflicting opinions have necessarily involved the subject in a good deal of confusion ; and statesmen still hold contrary opinions on the expediency of the brand, who would be unanimous in

* The Commission of 1866 consisted of Mr. (now Sir J.) Caird, Professor Huxley, and Mr. G. S. Lefevre, Sir J. Lefevre's son.

condemning the introduction of a similar system into any other branch of industry. The great and increasing importance of the trade, the circumstance that the brand places, or is supposed to place, the small curer on a level with the large one, the knowledge that branded herrings command a higher price in the German markets than unbranded herrings, are all confidently quoted as reasons for continuing the system; while the fact that the fees, charged for the brand, exceed the cost of the establishment which awards it, is cited as a conclusive argument for its retention.

These views, however, would be stated with less confidence if men would condescend to apply general principles of policy to this particular question. If it be a legitimate function of Government to guarantee by its brand the quality or quantity of a particular article, there is no reason whatever why the Ministry should draw the line at herrings. The Government used to undertake to guarantee the quality of cured cod; at an earlier period it actually stamped linen and woollen goods; and there is no very clear reason why if its action is justifiable in one case, it should not be extended to all industries. The advocates of the herring brand, indeed, declare that, as the purchaser is unable to examine for himself the quality of the herrings packed in the barrel, there is an exceptional reason for giving to him the guarantee which a Government brand affords. But it is obvious that the argument, if it has any cogency, is capable of almost indefinite extension. Take, for instance, the most important industry in which Englishmen are engaged. The Chinese complain that cotton goods are constantly adulterated by excessive or impure sizing. Will the Government undertake to guarantee that every bale of cotton goods is free from improper sizing ? The cotton manufacturers might very possibly undertake to pay a small fee for the privilege of such a guarantee, and the Government might consequently obtain a remunerative duty. The folly of such a course would, however, at once prevent its adoption. Government, it would be said, has nothing to do with the manufacturers. It must leave them to attend to their own business, and to bear the consequences of their own errors ; or, if they are dishonest enough to commit them, to suffer the penalty which sooner or later attends fraudulent practices.

Nor is it quite clear that the brand does afford the guarantee which it is its whole object to supply. Complaints of the bad quality of branded herrings occasionally reach Scotland from German buyers. Those who desire to see the complaints themselves will find samples of them in the "Appendix to the Report of the Select Committee on the Herring Brand." It was broadly stated to that Committee that the brand was awarded to a low average of cure ; it was stated that even this average was not maintained. Its existence, therefore, was alleged to discourage improvement, and to afford no real protection to the curer.

It is said, however, that the brand has the effect of placing the small curer on a level with the large one ; and that its abolition would give an advantage to the large capitalist whose private brand would be known, and so tend to ruin the smaller one. It is an obvious reflection that this argument, if it be sound, is applicable to other industries besides that of the curer ; but it is equally evident that it is no part of the function of Government to try to remove the advantageous distinctions which men have secured from their own industry or from their own skill. If a large curer has from his success succeeded in obtaining a certain reputation for his own fish, it is not just that he should be deprived of the advantage which he is entitled to derive from the pains which he has taken, or that he should be placed on a level with other and less successful men. Protection to the small curer may too often mean protection to the less energetic tradesman.

But there is another and a graver objection to the continuance of the brand. Any government guarantee necessarily implies conformity with certain prescribed conditions. The brand has, therefore, the effect of stereotyping the trade and preventing improvement. The herrings must be packed in specified barrels, made in one particular way ; they must be cured in a prescribed manner and mixed with a given proportion of salt. If an intelligent curer ventures to think that he can improve the process, he must do so at the certain risk of losing the brand, and so of lowering the value of his fish. If even, as happened in the great fishing of 1880, the stock of available barrels is exhausted, the curers are unable to supplement the deficiency by using Norwegian barrels, since their use would not entitle them to the brand. Everything, in fact, must be done by rule ; every departure from regulation must be followed by a pecuniary loss to the curer, and the trade, in consequence, is carried on, year after year, in the same unvarying manner, with a Conservative aversion from change, which would be worthy of the Chinese Empire.

Nor is there any reason for assuming that the trade would, in any sense, suffer from the abolition of the brand. In the first place there is no brand on the west coast of Scotland ; and there is a large trade between the west coast of Scotland and the Continent in "matties,"* or young herrings cured. In the next place, the brand does

* Mattie is a Dutch word ; it signifies, literally, maiden.

not fulfil the purposes for which it was designed. It has been already stated that the Continental buyers occasionally complain that they buy branded herrings which are not of a quality that would entitle them to the brand. It is difficult to see how any other result could happen. The duty of the fishery officers, who award the brand, becomes more difficult precisely as the take becomes larger ; and, however zealous the officers may be, it is impossible for them to see all the contents of every barrel.* The brand, therefore, occasionally covers bad articles. It might be possible to argue that a brand, which proved the quality of the fish as accurately as the stamp of the Mint proves the quality and quantity of the gold in a sovereign, served a useful purpose. It is difficult to see what advantage can ensue from a brand which does not and cannot fulfil this object. It is a mere wanton restriction on the curer, which should be got rid of at the first opportunity.

It is remarkable too that this conclusion, still stoutly resisted in Scotland and Parliament, has already been accepted by other nations. Some years ago Norwegian herrings were regularly branded ; and in 1856 Admiral Sullivan, the member of the Commission of 1855, who dissented from the conclusions of the majority of its members, wrote of Norwegian herrings that " with the

---

* The fishery officers are required to test the quality of the fish by opening a certain proportion of the barrels presented for the brand at the rate of

    9 barrels per hundred in parcels of 100 barrels.

    8   ,,   ,,   ,,   from 100 to 300 barrels.

    7   ,,   ,,   ,,   of above 300 barrels.

The barrels selected for examination are, as a general rule, to be opened alternately ; *i.e.* No. 1 is to be opened at the head end : No. 2 at the bottom end, and so on.—Report Select Committee on Herring Brand, p. 253.

exception of a small and unimportant portion, they are
so inferior in quality when caught that no mode of cure
will enable them to compete on equal terms with the
Scotch, which appear to have the entire command of the
principal German and Polish markets." Since these words
were written the brand or "brack," as it is called in Norway,
has fallen into disuse; and the Norwegian herrings now
constitute the principal supply, and command the highest
prices in the German markets. So plain a lesson, which
has not yet been learned by statesmen in England, has not
been lost on the Dutch, who, in their turn, have abolished
the brand. The striking fact, therefore, remains that
this country, which had the distinction of initiating free
trade, is the only nation having an important fish trade
which still clings to an obsolete and vicious system. The
fishery continues to flourish; but it flourishes in spite of,
not in consequence of, the brand.

It is perhaps necessary to add that the brand affixed to
the barrel is supposed to indicate the quality of the fish.
The highest brand is awarded to what are technically called
crown full herrings, that is large herrings full of roe, care-
fully gutted with a knife. The next highest brand is given
to crown matties, a "maiden" fish—that is, smaller herrings
with minute roes. Shotten herrings, or herrings which have
cast their roe, are branded as crown spent; while herrings
of all these qualities, packed in the same barrel, are branded
crown mixed. The barrel contains 26⅔ imperial gallons,
or 32 gallons English wine measure.

It has been already stated that the chief market for
Scotch herrings is found in the Protestant States of
Germany; but a large number of herrings cured in a
different way are sold in the United Kingdom. These
consist of red herrings, kippered herrings, and bloaters.

D

Red herrings are fish which after being kept in the salt pickle from two to fourteen days, are washed, dried, hung up in the smoking-house on spits, and smoked with oak or ash smoke for ten or fourteen days more. Kippered herrings, after being salted, are cut open and slightly smoked ; while bloaters are the best fish that can be procured, smoked for a much shorter period. Red herrings are usually packed in barrels or boxes, and are either exported or sold in the large towns. In this country, however, they are perhaps gradually being superseded by the kipper and the bloater ; and a large and increasing trade is continually being conducted in these two kinds of cured fish.*

In addition, however, to the trade in cured herrings, large and increasing numbers of herrings are annually sold fresh. The railways, in fact, by ensuring a rapid delivery, have enabled fish to be sold fresh, which half a century ago could not possibly have reached the fish markets in good order. The fish which are caught on the English, Manx, and Irish coasts, are to a great extent disposed of in this way ; and fresh herrings form one of the cheapest kinds of animal food procurable in the United Kingdom.

Herrings are measured in Scotland by the cran. A cran contains thirty-six gallons and holds from about 800 to 1000

---

* The colour is given to the red herring—which is occasionally a yellow herring—by the fuel with which it is smoked ; by altering the fuel the curer can alter the colour of the cured fish. Perhaps few people know that the term kipper is derived from the kype or hook on the lower jaw of the spawning male salmon. The male salmon from this kype became known as the kipper. The male fish was usually cured, and known as kipper salmon. The term was soon corrupted into kippered salmon, and the word "kipper" turned into a verb became synonymous with to cure. Bloaters are an invention of the present century.

herrings. A barrel of full herrings contains 700 to 750 fish. As, however, a certain proportion of herrings is unsuitable for the curer, probably one cran of herrings must be caught for every barrel of herrings that is cured. In other words, about 1,000,000,000 herrings must be annually caught in Scotland for the purposes of the curer. Assuming that only one herring is sold fresh in Scotland for every four that are cured, the surprising number of 1,250,000,000 of herrings must be annually taken in Scotland. In Ireland and the Isle of Man herrings are measured by the mease, which contains 525 fish ; and the Irish fishery, according to the Irish Inspectors, produces from about 50,000 to about 200,000 mease a year, or from about 25,000,000 to about 100,000,000 fish a year. In England, herrings are usually sold by the last, each last nominally containing 10,000, but in reality 13,200 fish.* It is impossible to give any accurate statistics of the yield of the English Herring Fishery. But it will, perhaps, be reasonable to assume that its produce is half as great as that of the Scotch fishery. In other words, that it yields 600,000,000 or 625,000,000 of fish a year. It is probable, therefore, that British fishermen draw nearly 2,000,000,000 herrings annually from the British seas. The value of these fish, placing them at a farthing apiece, must exceed £2,000,000.

From a naturalist's point of view, sprats, or "garvies," as they are called in Scotland, are closely connected with herrings. They are caught in enormous quantities in the estuary of the Thames and in the estuaries of eastern Scotland. It is said that as much as 200 tons of these fish

* The Last, a German word, is computed in this way :—
4 herrings = 1 warp.
33 warps = 1 hundred.
10 hundred = 1 thousand.

have been brought to London in a single day ; and they are sold wholesale in London by the bushel for from 2*s.* to 8*s.* They are so numerous that it is frequently impossible to dispose of them for food ; and large quantities are occasionally sold at a still lower price as manure.   The season for sprat fishing commences early in November and lasts for about three months.   No food equally nutritious is ever procurable at so cheap a rate by the poor.   If sprats were only as dear as salmon, perhaps no food would be more prized on the table of the rich.

No available means exist for determining the value of the Sprat fisheries : the same thing is true of Whitebait.   The Whitebait of commerce consist of a variety of small fish ; but chiefly of young sprats and young herrings.   They are mainly caught in the estuaries of the Thames and of the Medway, but they are found on almost every part of the British coasts, and fisheries for them are gradually springing up in various places.   They are commonly sold in London at about 1*s.* a quart, and are thus included among the cheaper kinds of fish.   The destruction of them year after year is enormous ; and there is perhaps no better proof of the marvellous fertility of the sea than may be deduced from the circumstance that the continuous destruction of whitebait is making no impression whatever on the supply either of sprats or of herrings.

The Mackerel fishery is conducted in many places by the same boats and by the same fishermen as the herring fishery.   Its importance has gained for the fish a singular exemption.   By an old act of Charles II., which is still in force, no wares, goods, fruit, herbs and chattels, may be sold on Sunday.   By an act of George III., which is also on the Statute Book, fish brought to London on Saturday night is expressly ordered to be publicly sold on Monday morning.

But a different rule is applied to mackerel, and permission is given for its sale either before or after Divine Service on Sunday. The distinction probably arose from the conviction that a rich oily fish like the mackerel, which commonly reached London in hot summer weather, could not be kept fresh for the additional twenty-four hours. The strict observance of the Sabbath, however desirable it might be, could not compensate for the loss of valuable food. Mackerel used usually to be taken in the English and in the Bristol channels, but of late years a large fishery for this fish has sprung up at Kinsale in the south of Ireland. The fishery is attended by English, Scotch, Manx, and Irish boats, and is every year extending further and further round the south-west coast. The Irish inspectors compute the value of the mackerel caught off the coast of Kerry and Cork at nearly £150,000, but a further sum must be added to this amount for the fish taken off the coast of Clare. It is probable that the Irish mackerel fishery thus produces a gross sum of £175,000 annually : if the whole of the Channel fisheries for mackerel is only of the same value as those off the Irish coast, the mackerel fishery of the British Islands must be worth £350,000 annually.

Thus the drift fishermen, fishing for surface fish, are dependent for their harvest on herrings, mackerel, sprats, and pilchards.* If the yield of the herring fishery may be placed at £2,000,000 ; that of the mackerel fishery at £350,000 ; that of the pilchard fishery at £50,000—£36,000, for the foreign, and £14,000 for the home trade—it will

* These fish are not, of course, solely caught with drift nets. Herrings in Loch Fyne are caught with a ground seine net ; or, as it is locally termed, a trawl net. Pilchards are also largely, and mackerel occasionally, caught with seines. Sprats are caught with seines in some places, and in stow boat nets in the estuary of the Thames.

perhaps, be justifiable to assume that these fisheries and
the fishery for young sprats and young herrings, known as
whitebait, yield to the fishermen a gross revenue of from
£2,500,000 to £2,750,000 a year. This sum, which is
purposely computed in the most moderate manner, repre-
sents the value of the fish on the coast, and not its much
higher value in the markets.

Before proceeding to deal with the great line and trawl
fisheries which form the main source of the fish supply, it
may be convenient to add a few words on the fisheries for
migratory fish. There are four kinds of migratory fish which
are taken in this country : Salmon, including in the term
all migratory fish of the family; smelts, the *éperlan* of France,
or the sparling of northern England ; shad or twait, and
eels ; of these, salmon are by far the most important.
They are caught by fixed nets on the coasts of Scotland,
and by fixed engines in the rivers, by seine-nets, or by net and
coble, to use the Scotch term for a seine-net ; and by drift-
nets off the coast of Northumberland and in some parts of
Ireland. The Irish Salmon Fisheries are estimated to yield
£579,000 a year. This estimate, however, has been made by
computing the value of the fish at 1s. 6d. a lb. Placing
it at the more moderate price of 1s. a lb., the yield of these
fisheries may be estimated at about £400,000. The value
of the Scotch salmon fisheries is certainly not less than
£250,000 annually, and probably reaches £300,000. The
yield of the English Salmon Fisheries has been frequently
computed at £100,000 a year.

It seems, therefore, not unreasonable to assume that the
salmon fisheries of the British Islands yield to the fishermen
some £800,000 annually. It is perhaps fair to suppose that
the fisheries for other migratory fish—eels, twait, and smelts
—produce at least £100,000 a year. If then the value of

the drift fisheries and of the analogous fisheries for pilchards, sprats and whitebait, may be placed at from £2,500,000 to £2,750,000, and that of the fisheries for migratory fish at £900,000, it is a safe and moderate estimate to compute the produce of the whole of these fisheries at £3,500,000 annually.

These fisheries, however, important as they are, bear no comparison with the great fishery for bottom fish, which used to be exclusively taken by lines, but which are now chiefly captured by trawl-nets.   It is no exaggeration to say that London and the great centres of population are dependent for their supply of fish on trawlers ; and that if, from any cause whatever, trawling were suddenly terminated, its termination would be followed by famine in the fish market. No clear history of trawl-fishing has ever yet been written ; and its origin is uncertain.   There are, however, many reasons for believing that trawling, to a limited extent, has been practised for centuries in Britith waters, and that trawlers worked in Torbay in the reign of Elizabeth.

Trawling, however, if it were practised by our ancestors, was chiefly confined to Devonshire, and was carried on in only a humble fashion.   The vast extension of this mode of fishing did not take place till our own time.   Till, indeed, railways were invented the present system was impossible, since no means were available for carrying the tons of fish, which were thus caught daily, from the ports to the markets. Trawling is now carried on off almost all the coasts of this country.   The Fleetwood trawlers work in Morecambe Bay, the Liverpool trawlers on the smooth bottom of the sea between the Isle of Man and Lancashire, while they occasionally leave their ordinary grounds and go as far south as Aberystwyth.   The Brixham trawlers working mainly in Torbay and Mount's Bay also frequently visit the

Bristol Channel, while Dover, Ramsgate, Hastings, Rye, and other ports all contribute their trawlers to the English Channel.

But the main home of trawling at the present time is to be found in the ports which fringe the North Sea, and it is no exaggeration to say that these ports form the most important fishing stations, and the North Sea the most productive fishery, in the world. Most people have some acquaintance with the shape of the North Sea. It is comparatively small, it is shallow, and it is surrounded on three sides by the different countries of Europe which are watered by large rivers. All these conditions are favourable for the production of fish of a high quality. The rivers bring down from the adjacent land a vast quantity of minute life which forms the food of young fish; the sandy *plateaux* which fringe the shores are the nurseries for the fry; while the deeper depressions, which are to be found here and there in the bottom of the sea, afford shelter for the mature fish in cold and stormy weather. The gulf stream is unable to force its way into the basin of this sea, and its waters are consequently colder than those of the Bristol Channel and the Irish Sea. Its colder waters, though unfavourable for mackerel and a few other fish, improve the quality as food of its cod, its haddock, and its other habitants.

The bottom of the sea resembles the surface of the land. It is an undulating pasture intersected by valleys in some places and hills in others. The submarine slopes and depressions in the North Sea are not indeed very great. The hills and valleys, like those of Eastern England, are of moderate height and depth, and there are few if any places in it, south of the 55th parallel, which are more than 300 feet deep. Just as the shepherd drives his flocks in summer to the hills and in winter to the valleys, so in summer the fish frequent the sandy elevated *plateaux* beneath the sea, while in winter they withdraw into the deeper submarine depressions. The sandy or muddy eminences in which the fish are found in summer fringe the coasts of England, Holland, Germany, and Denmark. But in addition to the elevations which surround the basin of the sea, a great block of high tableland, about 200 miles long and about 30 miles broad, runs from south-west to north-east almost in the middle of the sea. This is the Dogger Bank where, rather more than a hundred years ago, Dutch and English fought a sharp and indecisive action, and where now hundreds of British, Dutch, and French fishermen obtain a livelihood. In the immediate vicinity of the south of the Dogger, the land abruptly slopes away into a valley which was probably once a river estuary, and which is now known as the outer Silver Pit ; while south of this again the southern shore of the old watercourse is formed by some elevated ground known as the Well Bank. Between the Well Bank and the English coast the high tableland is intersected by two deep depressions, known as the Sole Pit and the Silver Pit. North-west of these again, the stony foreshore which runs from Flamborough Head bears the name of California.

These salient features in the physical aspect of the North Sea ought to be understood by any one who desires to form a clear idea of the fishing trade of the United Kingdom. The names which, in modern times, have been given to some of these submarine valleys and hills, such as the Silver Pit, the outer Silver Pit, and California, sufficiently indicate the importance which fishermen attach to the grounds. In cold weather, indeed, the flat fish are congregated together in the valleys and fall an easy prey to the trawler ; and the chief fishing port of the United Kingdom, Grimsby, owes its origin and prosperity to the fact that it is immediately adjacent to the Silver Pit.

This fact is so curious that it is worth while to trace the rise of Grimsby during the last half century. Rather more than fifty years ago, Grimsby is said to have owned one fishing-boat. In 1843 the Silver Pit was first worked, but it was worked by Brixham and other vessels coming to the port. But the trade, when it once began, rapidly developed. The Manchester and Sheffield Railway was carried into the port. Large sums of money were spent in building docks, the fishing fleet increased by " leaps and bounds," till, in 1881, the port, which in 1830 had possessed one boat, owned 607 vessels registering 35,000 tons, and employing nearly 4000 persons.

The North Sea trawlers follow two systems of fishing. Some of them, fishing the adjacent grounds, return constantly to port, and send their fish direct by railway to London or to other populous towns ; others of them repair in fleets to the distant grounds, and are absent from home for weeks at a time. In consequence of their prolonged absence they in turn have created a fresh industry. Steamers are employed to repair to the fleet and take the fish which have been caught from the boats, and carry them to England. Boats for this purpose ply from Hull, from Grimsby, and from London. The fish are carried from the smack to the steamer in open boats, and some loss of life unfortunately results from this ferrying trade. No means, however, have yet been invented of transferring the fish from the smack to the steamer without the assistance of the small open boats.

In addition to the legitimate trade of carrying the fish from the fleet to the market, another more objectionable

system has of late years sprung up in the fishing fleet.
When men are absent from home for long periods, they
require to be supplied with various articles ; and, in consequence of the demand which has thus sprung up, smacks
have been fitted out for the sale to the fishing fleet of
spirits, tobacco, and other things. As these smacks buy
their goods abroad, and do not return to a British port
before they are sold, they naturally escape the customs
duties, and are consequently able to sell spirits and tobacco
at the lowest possible rate. Cheap drink is perhaps always
objectionable, and an unregulated liquor traffic is usually
liable to abuse. The boat-owners complain that the
coopers, as these smacks are called, are floating grog-shops
of the worst description, and that they are under no control
whatever. They demoralise the fishermen and tempt them
to part with fish and gear for spirits and tobacco. It is
not, however, easy to see how these evils, great as they are,
can effectually be terminated. If coopering were forbidden
in English vessels, the only result would be to drive the
trade under a foreign flag. The true method of terminating
abuse probably consists in endeavouring to make the trade
itself more respectable. If the boat-owners would encourage
smacks sailing under proper control, and dealing not merely
in spirits but in coffee and other necessaries, to attend the
fleet, the respectable trade might perhaps in the long run
destroy the disreputable one. If people will not condescend
to supply a well-ascertained demand in a regular way,
irregular means of meeting it are certain to arise.

It is not very easy to obtain any reliable statistics of the
value of the trawling trade. The same ports which own
the chief trawlers own the chief smacks engaged in the line
trade ; and the fish which both classes of vessels produce
are consequently sold through the same markets. Nearly

75,000 tons of fish are, however, sent away annually by
railway from Hull and Grimsby alone.   It is, perhaps, a
fair assumption that for every three tons brought away from
Grimsby by land, one ton is either carried direct from the
smacks to London or sold in the neighbourhood.   If this
assumption is accurate, some 100,000 tons of fish must be
annually caught by the Hull and Grimsby boats.   Placing
the value of these fish at the ports at rather less than
2*d.* a lb., or £20 a ton, the smacks of these ports must
annually obtain fish worth £2,000,000.   It is almost certain
that the fish caught by lines and trawls in all the other
ports of the kingdom exceed in quantity the fish caught
by the trawlers of Hull and Grimsby alone.   If it is only
equal to the quantity caught by the boats of these two
ports the trawl and line fish of the British Islands must be
worth £4,000,000 annually.

Thus, if the estimates in the foregoing pages be reliable,
it is possible to form some idea of the value of the fishing
industry of the British Islands.   It was shown on an early
page of this essay that merely testing it by the value of the
capital employed and the number of fishermen engaged, it
was probable that the fishery produced from £9,000,000 to
£10,000,000 a year.   It has now been shown specifically
that the trawl and line fisheries in all probability yield
£4,000,000, the herring fishery £2,000,000, the salmon
fishery £800,000, the mackerel fishery £350,000, and that
the fisheries for pilchards, whitebait, and smelts bring up
these totals to at least £7,500,000 annually.   To these
must be added the fisheries for fish, which, strictly speaking, are not fish, for crustaceans, such as lobsters, crabs,
prawns, and shrimps : and for molluscs, such as oysters,
mussels, whelks, and winkles.

It is no easy matter to give any estimate, which is worth

publishing, of the value of these fisheries. It is stated in the last edition of the "Encyclopœdia Britannica" that 2000 gallons of shrimps a day are sent away occasionally from Leigh in Essex. Assuming that the whole annual catch is only fifty times the catch of a single day, 100,000 gallons of shrimps must be taken at Leigh alone. Their value, at 1*s.* a gallon, would be £5,000 a year. But Leigh is not the only or the chief home of the fishery. Wherever a sandy shore fringes the coast shrimpers are at work, and their gross take must be very large. If it be only twenty times the take at Leigh, it must amount to £100,000 annually. Perhaps it will surprise still more persons to learn that the cockles which are gathered in Morecambe Bay are sold for at least £20,000 a year,* and that more than 2,500 tons of periwinkles are annually consumed in London. Yet Morecambe Bay is not the only place in which cockles yield a fertile harvest to the neighbourhood, and London is not the only large town where people buy periwinkles by the ton load. Shrimps, cockles, and periwinkles form, however, only a small portion of the trade in shell fish. The more important portions of this trade are the trade in mussels, the trade in lobsters and crabs, and the trade in oysters.

More than thirty years ago, according to a return which was published by the Deep Sea Fishery Commissioners of 1866,† 498,000,000 oysters, or, in round numbers, 500,000,000 oysters were sold in London. Placing them at only a halfpenny apiece, and omitting the large quantities sold on the coast and other places, the value of the oysters sold must have exceeded £1,000,000. There is reason for fearing that the continual decrease of oysters during the last quarter of a century must have diminished these sales. But, if the number has decreased, the price has increased ;

* See "Fisheries Comm.," 1879, p. 238. † P. 457.

and the total value of the smaller quantity of oysters sold now must be at least as great as that of the larger quantity of oysters sold thirty years ago. If, however, the oysters alone are worth £1,000,000, it is not a very excessive estimate to presume that the other shell fish—lobsters, crabs, prawns, shrimps, mussels, cockles, whelks, and winkles—produce another £1,000,000. In other words, while the fish taken off our coasts yield some £7,500,000 annually, the shell fish raise the total yield of the harvest of the sea to £9,500,000.

These figures, it will be seen, agree with the original estimate based on the number of fishermen employed, and on the estimated capital embarked in the fisheries. And, if attention be paid to another portion of the trade, it will be seen that the calculation is further corroborated. Hitherto this essay has dealt chiefly with the catching of the fish; but no account of the fish trade would be complete without some explanation of the manner in which the fish caught are distributed. The distribution is effected in four ways: (1) The largest proportion of the fish caught is conveyed inland by railway to the great markets; (2) a further proportion is carried to the markets by sea or river; (3) large quantities of fish are exported; and (4) considerable numbers of fish are consumed near the ports where they are taken.

In 1881, 206,000 tons of fish were conveyed inland by railway from the English ports, 59,000 tons were conveyed inland from the Scotch ports, and 7000 tons were conveyed inland from the Irish ports. The fish sent away from the various ports by train amounted in the aggregate to 272,000 tons. If the value of the fish is placed at £20 a ton, the fish so carried must have been worth £5,440,000; 42,000 tons of fish were carried direct from the sea to

Billingsgate ; estimating them again at £20 a ton, the total value of the fish carried by railway to inland towns, and by water to Billingsgate, must be worth £6,280,000. It has been already shown that the value of the fish exported exceeds £1,820,000 a year. It is possible, therefore, accurately to account for fish worth £8,100,000. If it be recollected that Liverpool, one of the most important fish markets in the country, is largely supplied by water, that Shields, Edinburgh, and, to a certain extent, Glasgow, are also supplied by water, and that all round the coasts a population—counted by tens of thousands. in the summer season—is consuming fish, it seems not unfair to assume that another £1,000,000 or £1,500,000 worth of fish may be accounted for, and that the gross yield of the fisheries may again be raised to £9,000,000 or £10,000,000 a year.

There are several points connected with these figures which are well worth attention. The first circumstance which will strike everyone is the insignificance of the yield of the Irish fisheries. Only 7,000 tons of fish were conveyed inland by Irish railways. It is true that large quantities of fish are taken direct from the Irish ports to Holyhead and Milford ; but, if it be assumed that the whole of the fish taken inland from these two ports was Irish, the Irish fisheries will still only supply 20,000 tons of fish to the markets. The Irish fishermen are mainly engaged in supplying the home markets ; the Scotch fishermen are largely occupied in supplying the foreign markets ; and yet Ireland only sends one ton of fish to the home markets for every three tons which the Scotch fisheries, after complying with the requirements of a great foreign trade, are able to consign to them. It may be thought that the situation of Ireland, its distance from London, and the intervening channel are responsible for this state of things. But there are islands on the west of Scotland which are as remote from the markets as Ireland itself. The Western Hebrides, till lately, sent their fish to London either by Glasgow or by Strome Ferry. In 1880 the opening of the Oban railway gave them a new outlet for their industry; and, in 1881, upwards of 12,000 tons of fish were despatched from Oban alone by railway, while upwards of 1,000 tons were sent from Strome Ferry. The remote islands, which are known as the outer Hebrides, are probably, therefore, sending two tons of fish to the British markets for every three tons that arrive from the whole of Ireland.

The desultory operations of the Irish fishermen will be still better understood if the figures are examined in another way. The 42,000 fishermen of England and Wales despatch to the home and foreign markets 260,000 tons of fish, or about six tons for each fisherman. The 48,000 Scotch fishermen send about 60,000 tons of fish to the home markets, and about 100,000 tons of fish to the foreign markets, or nearly 4 tons to each fisherman. But the 24,000 Irish fishermen only send away about 20,000 tons of fish, or less than 1 ton for each fisherman: and these figures, striking as they are, do not, it must be recollected, represent the whole truth.* A large proportion of the Irish fish are not caught by Irish fishermen, but by Scotch, Manx, and English fishing-boats. A large proportion of the English and Scotch fish, moreover, is consumed on the coasts, while there is no large consumption of fish on the Irish coasts.

These facts will appear still more remarkable if they be

---

* In the preceding figures I have assumed (1) that all the herrings exported were exported from Scotland; (2) that 10 barrels of herrings weigh 1 ton; (3) that all the other fish exported were exported from England. I have computed this at 22,000 tons.

compared with the statistics for Wales. Irish fishermen have been the favourite object of state patronage for years : so long as this patronage continues there will always be a race of Irish fishermen. But no politician has yet risen up who has demanded state patronage for Welsh fishermen ; and in consequence, the Welsh fisheries can hardly be said to exist at all. If Holyhead and Milford be excluded, the whole of the Welsh ports did not send 1,000 tons of fish by railway to the markets in 1881. Yet North Wales on a clear day can look upon the hills of the Isle of Man, which has nurtured the hardiest race of fishermen in the world ; South Wales is not much more distant from the opposite coasts of Cornwall whose people draw a rich harvest from the sea ; while in West Wales stranger boats pursue a profitable herring fishery. It is almost an inevitable deduction from these facts that the Welsh and Irish fisheries do not prosper because the Welsh and Irish people do not take readily to sea-fishing as a pursuit.

Of the 272,000 tons of railway-borne fish, which were carried inland in 1881, about 90,000 tons were brought to London. The Metropolis, therefore, in addition to the large quantities of fish which it received direct from the sea, absorbed one-third of the whole of the fish carried inland by railway. The supply of fish to London has been steadily increasing for several years ; rising from about 95,000 tons in 1875, to about 130,000 tons in 1880. Out of this vast supply of 130,000 tons, more than three-fourths, or 100,000 tons, were drawn from the North Sea. London, however, is not the only market which is dependent on the North Sea. Out of the 206,000 tons of fish which are borne annually from English ports by railways, 164,000 tons are carried from ports situated on the North Sea. The North Sea, therefore, is the main source of the fish supply of the United

E

Kingdom, and its fisheries are more productive than many countries. If it be recollected, indeed, that in addition to British fishermen, its waters are fished by Norwegian, Danish, German, Dutch, Belgian and French fishermen, some idea will perhaps be formed of the fertility of this sea. It is probable that fishermen extract from its waters every year fish worth £25,000,000.

It must not be supposed that the whole of the fish brought to London are consumed in the Metropolis. On the contrary, London is the central source of the supply of a district which every year tends to become larger. One of the most certain consequences of improved locomotion is the concentration of trade. It is found practically more convenient for buyers and sellers to meet in one place than to scatter themselves among a great many places. In nothing is this tendency more perceptible than in the fish trade. London and Birmingham, and, to a lesser extent, Manchester and Liverpool, are the markets from which nearly the whole of England is supplied with fish ; and London is annually becoming to a greater extent the centre of the supply. Gentlemen residing in distant counties have their dish of fish regularly sent to them by a London tradesman : fishmongers in provincial towns receive their fish uniformly from Billingsgate ; and Billingsgate is thus becoming a central fish exchange for the whole country.

This state of things could not have arisen except from two circumstances. In the first place, the development of the railway system has enabled large and small parcels of goods to be despatched at a comparatively slight cost to distant places ; and, in the next place, the importation and the manufacture of ice have made it possible to keep perishable goods from decay during transit. As distributors of fish, the railways would have lost half their utility without ice ; while ice, as a preservative, would have been too heavy for the old conveyances to have carried. Ice, as an article of commerce, has not had a history of fifty years. Before the development of railways and the trade in ice, fish were brought to London in welled smacks. The welled smacks are not even now entirely superseded. They are still used in the Grimsby line trade, and Dutch eels are brought to the Thames in the same way.* But the railway has become the great carrier of fish ; the railways bring the fish wholesale to Billingsgate ; they distribute them subsequently in small parcels throughout the country.

If these facts be borne in mind, it will be easily understood that space is eminently desirable at Billingsgate. A market which is already the centre of an enormous trade, and which every year is required to transact a larger business, must provide adequate accommodation for those who frequent it. Unfortunately Billingsgate does not fulfil these requirements. Built originally at a time when London was, compared with its present dimensions, a small town, and when the fish trade was only a humble undertaking, it is inadequate to supply the wants of the largest capital in the world. Nor is it easy to see how its shortcomings can be dealt with. Situated as it is in the centre of London, the surrounding land is occupied by property of a valuable

---

* There is a curious circumstance connected with the carriage of Dutch eels which is worth recording. The increasing pollution of the Thames made it impossible to bring even eels alive to London. " For ten years," so said Sir Robert Peel in the House of Commons in 1828, " the water was deteriorating in quality, as was found by various fishermen who had found it necessary to abandon this mode of obtaining a livelihood, in consequence of the insalubrity of the water driving away the fish. In truth, the fishermen's trade was destroyed ; and, strange to tell, eels imported from Holland would not live in Thames water."

character, and the expense of acquiring additional space in the immediate neighbourhood would strain the resources even of so wealthy a corporation as the Court of Common Council. This circumstance has induced some authorities to believe that the true way of relieving Billingsgate is to build a new wholesale market in another part of the city. The Corporation has actually, in the last few months, devoted to the fish trade, a market constructed for other purposes.

The reason commonly assigned for the construction of a second market is plausible. Part of the fish which London receives—so it is said—arrives by railway ; another portion of it comes by water. The railway-borne fish, it is argued, should be consigned to a market conveniently near to the termini of the great railways ; the river-borne fish should be sold in a market contiguous to the river. One class of fish should, therefore, be sent to a place like Smithfield ; the other class can continue to be disposed of in Billingsgate. This argument, plausible as it is, crumbles away when it is tested. What is a wholesale market ? It is obviously a place where buyers and sellers meet, and where all the operations of the trade should be concentrated. The ordinary tradesman, if he can get all his fish at one market, will not take the trouble or incur the expense of driving every morning to two markets. He will select one of the two markets, and to that market he will go ; and his selection will not depend on mere considerations of geography. The best fish reaches London by water. The tradesman who wishes to have the best possible turbot, for instance, on his slab, must go to the waterside market. But it is easy to see that, if this be true, the railway-borne fish will also go to the same market. The salesman at Aberdeen or at Grimsby will not consider which of the two markets

will be most accessible from Liverpool Street or King's
Cross ; he will simply ascertain which of the two markets is
attended by the retail tradesmen, and at which of the two
markets his fish will consequently command the best price.
No expenditure on the part of the Common Council will
induce the retail fishmonger to drive to Smithfield if he can
get all the fish which he requires at Billingsgate. It is
certain that he will be able to get fish at Billingsgate which
he will not get at Smithfield ; and to Billingsgate he will
accordingly go. The moment this is made plain to country
salesmen they will as a matter of course send all their fish
to Billingsgate ; and Billingsgate will thus be never superseded except by a new market on the waterside.

It does not, of course, follow from this reasoning that it is
inexpedient to establish other fish markets in other parts of
the Metropolis for the convenience of the retail trade. The
only possible argument against the institution of retail
markets seems to be that they are opposed to the habits of
the ordinary London householder who, as a rule, seems to
expect that his tradesman shall come to him, and that he
shall not be required to go to his tradesman. But the success which has attended the establishment of co-operative
stores proves that the householder, for the sake of an appreciable advantage, will change his habits ; and, if fish can
be bought more cheaply at a retail market than in a shop,
the householder in the long run will probably go to the
market. But a retail market of this description will depend
on the wholesale market for its daily supply. Its institution
will in no way remove the necessity for one wholesale
market.

What then are the requirements which a wholesale
market should possess, and does Billingsgate fulfil them ?
" A market does not deserve the name which does not

afford (1) accommodation for buyers and sellers; (2) standing room, and, where perishable articles are concerned, standing room under covered ways for the vans which are being unpacked; and (3) easy access." * The accommodation in Billingsgate itself is scanty; but it is perhaps sufficient. The accommodation outside the market is disgracefully insufficient. The vans which bring the fish into it are forced to stand while they are unpacked in the. adjoining street; and this street which only extends along one side of the market is a narrow and inconvenient thoroughfare. The vans, therefore, are often delayed in their approach to the market, they are frequently forced to move on while vans with other fish for which there might be a greater demand at the moment are being brought up and unpacked, and these operations, which would be objectionable in any case, are doubly objectionable in the case of a perishable article like fish on a hot summer morning.

The time, therefore, has obviously arrived when the market and its approaches should be rendered adequate, or the market itself should be removed to some other situation. It must rest with the Corporation of London to determine which of the two courses should be taken. The Corporation owns the market, and is therefore the only body which can be expected to improve it. The reasons which make improvement preferable to removal must be plain to every one. Nothing is so conservative as trade, and nothing is so difficult as to alter the channel in which a particular trade flows. It may take time before any market, however convenient it may be, can supersede Billingsgate. On the other hand, the expense of making the approaches adequate for the trade is enormous. Bil-

---

* I have quoted in this paragraph a report of my own on the subject.

lingsgate stands on one of the most valuable sites in London. It is no exaggeration to say that unless its area is doubled, and Thames Street is broadened from end to end, all the necessary conditions of an adequate market will not be fulfilled. Improvements of such a character, however, will not cost merely thousands, or tens of thousands, but hundreds of thousands of pounds ; and it is for the Corporation to determine whether the game is worth the candle, or whether it would not be better to build at once a new market on another and new site at the waterside.

People who think hastily, or who do not think at all, usually suppose that the high price of fish in London is consequent on the inconvenience of Billingsgate ; and they frequently use the oddest of arguments to support their conclusions. Fish they say is cheap enough at Billingsgate, it may be purchased for 2*d.* per lb. ; but it is dear in the west end shops, and is not procurable for less than 8*d.* a lb. It may be doubted whether such statements as these have any real basis. Those who have most acquaintance with the case will hesitate to believe that the average price of all the fish sold at Billingsgate ever falls so low as 2*d.* per lb., or that the average price of all the fish sold by retail in London ever rises so high as 8*d.* Large as the profits of the retailers may be, they are not so large as common rumour supposes. If, however, the price of fish in west end shops is high, it is certain that the crowded streets of Billingsgate is not solely responsible for it. If the inconveniences of the market enhanced the price, it is obvious that they would raise the price in Billingsgate itself. They can have no effect on the price when the fish has once passed into the hands of the retailer. The whole gist of the ordinary complaint, however, is that

fish is cheap at Billingsgate and dear when it reaches the
consumer's hands ; and it is plain, therefore, that if the
complaint is well founded the cause must be sought outside
of the market.

It may, under the circumstances, be worth while to
consider what are some of the causes which legitimately
raise the price of fish to the consumer. It has hitherto
been assumed in this paper that the fishermen on an
average receive £20 a ton, or rather less than 2*d*. a lb.
for the fish which they catch ; but it must be recollected that this average price is computed from a great
many items. The average price of salmon for instance
exceeds 1*s*. per lb. ; the average price of sprats on the
coast is represented by a fraction of 1*d*. a lb. It cannot,
under such circumstances, be possible to state the average
value of all fish with anything like precision ; but the estimate of 2*d*. a lb. is perhaps sufficiently accurate. It
requires very little reflection to perceive that this sum must
be largely increased before the fish reach the hands of the
consumer. In the first place the fish are sold on the coasts
by a salesman ; they are packed in the railway vans ; in
hot weather they are packed in ice ; the railway freight
from the ports to London has to be paid ; the carriage
from the railway terminus to Thames Street has to be
charged ; the porterage from the van to the market has to
be added ; market dues at Billingsgate raise the price still
further ; the salesman at Billingsgate necessarily expects
his own profit ; and, lastly, the retailer has to charge his
own expenses in driving to the market to buy his fish, the
rent of his shop, and the cost of distributing the fish to the
consumer. In addition to all these expenses, a certain loss
must be experienced in dealing with a perishable article
like fish in hot weather. The price which the consumer

must pay, therefore, must be sufficient to cover this loss, and the retail price of fish must exceed and largely exceed the price received for it by the fishermen on the coasts.

It may perhaps be possible to place approximately this excess of cost in figures. The charges on the coast, for selling and packing the fish and for ice, may probably be placed at about £1 a ton, the cost of conveyance to London at £2 10s. to £3 a ton, the carriage to the market, porterage and market dues and the salesman's commission at another £1. The initial price, therefore, on the coast is raised from an average of £20 to an average of £24 10s., or £25 before the fish leaves the wholesale market. If the retailer's profits and his labour in going to and in carrying the fish from Billingsgate be placed at 25 per cent., the price will further be raised to £31 5s., and if a further 15s. be added to cover the cost of fish which either decays, or which is sold at a nominal price to prevent its decay, the average retail price will be raised from £20, the value of the fish on the coast, to £32, its price to the consumer.

This additional price, it must be recollected, would be much more serious in the case of the cheap fish which the trade, by a most unlucky name, calls "offal," * than with respect to the dear fish which are technically known as "prime." The transit charges, the market dues, the salesmen's commissions, and the expenses and a portion of the profits of the retailer would, in every case, have to be borne before the fish reached the consumer. If these charges reached on an average £10 or £11 a ton, they would repre-

---

* "Trawled fish is divided for market purposes into two classes, distinguished by the names of 'prime' and 'offal'; the former consisting of turbot, brill, soles, and dorys, and the latter of haddock, plaice, and other kinds of inferior fish "—Holdsworth's " Deep Sea Fishery," p. 15.

sent an addition of 1*d*. a lb. to the price ; and the fish, therefore, if they were given away on the shore, could not be retailed in London for less than a 1*d*. a lb.

It is no doubt true that one half of these charges could be avoided if the consumer went to Billingsgate and purchased his own fish ; and it is alleged that if Billingsgate were made more convenient and more accessible many con- sumers would take this course. But very little reflection will show that this course could not be taken by the ma- jority of householders. It must be a more inconvenient and costly thing for a householder to travel to Billingsgate for the sale of buying sixpennyworth of fish than to pay a tradesman a shilling for bringing the fish to his own door. Even then if the smaller householder could afford to pay as much as a 1*s*. for his fish, and the price of fish in the retail market was twice as much as its cost at Billingsgate, most people would find it cheaper and easier to employ a retail tradesman. The retailer, in fact, is carrying out the great principle of the subdivision of labour which is, in one sense, the cause and in another sense the consequence of modern progress ; and it would be absurd to suppose that his services could be dispensed with by a civilised com- munity.

Fish sold at Billingsgate are sold as a rule by auction. Fish sold on the coast in smaller ports, where there are no licensed auctioneers, are usually sold by what is called Dutch auction. On the coast the fish is generally bought by a buyer who is in direct communication with some firm at Billingsgate, which acts as the buyer's salesman. At Billingsgate the fish is either bought by the retailer direct, or by a middleman, who is known in the market as a " bomaree." The " bomaree " fulfils the same functions in the fish market which the " regrater " used to discharge in the corn market. He buys fish for which there is no immediate demand at the moment, and sells it again later on in the day. A good many people think that the interposition of the " bomaree " has the effect of further raising the price of fish and that it is therefore injurious. The clamour which Englishmen of another generation used to raise against the " regrater " is raised now against the " bomaree." The " bomaree," however, is really fulfilling a useful purpose. But for his intervention many small retail tradesmen would be forced to attend the market at an hour when their attendance would be inconvenient to them. The " bomaree " enables the small costermonger to postpone his visit to Billingsgate till he has disposed of his purchases of the previous day. Middlemen are never popular characters, yet the middleman, if his functions are examined, will generally be found to supply a public want, and to fulfil a useful purpose.

Such are some of the features in the trade of fish. An army of 120,000 persons is employed in catching them ; an army of 80,000 other persons probably find employment in curing them, or in other ways are dependent on the fishermen ; and an army of 10,000 to 20,000 persons is employed in selling them.

There is a singular distinction between the tastes of different parts of the community in respect to fish.* Some of the fish which the English eat are disliked by the Scotch, while the Scotch in their turn eat some fish which are not relished by the English. The Scotchman rarely eats a mackerel, and never eats an eel. He carries his dislike of

* The distaste of some nations for fish is remarkable. In the 12th Book of the Odyssey, Ulysses' companions would not eat fish till they were actually starving. Menelaus in the 4th Book says the same thing of his own companions ; and Plutarch declares that " among the Syrians and Greeks to abstain from fish was esteemed a piece of sanctity."

eels to such an extent that he does not even catch for the English market the eels with which many Scotch rivers abound. The herring, the haddock, and the salmon are the fish ordinarily found on Scotch tables ; and the haddock in Scotland almost fills the position which is occupied in England by the sole. On the other hand, Englishmen neglect many excellent kinds of fish. The pilchard, perhaps from the difficulty of carrying so oily a fish, rarely finds a market in England outside Cornwall. So excellent a fish as the halibut is not commonly eaten in London. The skate and the ling are comparatively seldom seen in the west end shops ; while the poorer classes, who eat cockles in Lancashire, and mussels in the Midland Counties, buy whelks and periwinkles in the London streets.

Perhaps, however, the most curious distinction between Scotch and English may be found in their respective preferences for the female and the male crab. In England the female crab is hardly saleable ; and probably the roe, which she carries inside her shell till it is ripe for extrusion, is chiefly used as dressing for turbot. In Scotland, on the contrary, the male crab is hardly ever eaten, and people will not buy a whole crab which is not a female. In the shops in Aberdeen the claws of the male crab are sold separately ; the bodies are frequently unsold. It would probably be difficult to find another instance, so marked, of the different habits or tastes of two people who are united in one nation by the tie of a common language and common interest.*

It has been the object of the preceding pages to describe

* In the same way the French send their lobsters to England ; while the cray fish of Cornwall find a rare market in London, and are sold in Paris. The "trout" of the Tweed (*salmo eriox*) would be rejected by any London epicure ; they command in the Paris market as high a price as salmon.

briefly the salient features of the fish trade of the United Kingdom. With this purpose an attempt has been made to show how fish are caught, to estimate the amount of capital embarked in the fisheries, the extent of the employment which they afford, and the value of the food which they produce. The fish have subsequently been followed from the markets to the consumer; and the manner in which their distribution is effected has been described. This account, however, would be hardly complete if it were to stop at this point. Most people who pay any attention to the subject of fisheries, are occupied rather with the future than with the present condition of the industry. It is hardly possible to take up a paper, or to hear a conversation which relates to fishery matters, without listening to or reading gloomy anticipations of the approaching exhaustion of the fish of the sea; and it is therefore necessary before concluding these pages to make a few remarks on this part of the subject.

And, in the first place, people do not seem to be aware that the predictions which are freely hazarded of the approaching exhaustion of the sea are not new. They are almost as old as English literature. Three hundred and thirty years ago a Bishop of St. David's declared that the scarcity of herrings was due to the covetousness of fishers, who in times of plenty took so many that they destroyed the breeders. The good Bishop who pronounced this positive opinion was burnt shortly afterwards at Carmarthen for heresy. But his opinions on fishery questions survived his martyrdom; and a few years afterwards Parliament complained that "in divers places they fed swine and dogs with the fry and spawn of fish; and otherwise, lamentable and horrible to be reported, destroy the same, to the great hindrance and decay of the Commonwealth." "Lamentable and horrible to be reported " the destruction continued, notwithstanding the action of the Legislature ; and it occurred to another Bishop that, as Parliamentary action had failed, recourse might be had to a Higher Power. Bishop Wilson, probably convinced like all around him of the decay of the fishery, added a paragraph to the Litany, and desired his clergy to pray every Sunday to God to *restore* the blessings of the sea. But though the prayer was offered up and abundantly answered, the same complaints continued. A few years afterwards, according to Mr. Lecky, the Irish fisheries decayed in consequence of the introduction of trawling on the Irish coast ; while, to come down to our own time, in the year in which the Queen ascended the throne, a petition presented to Parliament declared that the fishermen of Scotland, Ireland, and Holland had found out the breeding places of the herrings, and had resorted there to catch them, and that since the discovery was made the fish generally, throughout the west and north of Scotland, had annually decreased. What would the good Bishop of St. David's have said, 330 years ago, if some seer had told him that the time was coming when British fishermen would draw 2,000,000,000 herrings annually from the British seas, and that the fisheries would still go on increasing ? What would Parliament have said in 1558 if it had known that the " lamentable and horrible " practices which it denounced would be continued for upwards of three centuries, and that at the end of that time the British fisheries would yield a produce twenty times as valuable as the revenue which Elizabeth had at her disposal ? What would Parliament have said in 1837 if some statesman had used such language as this : This fishery which you declare is being destroyed, has never yet produced 500,000 barrels of cured herrings a year ; a little more than forty years hence it will regularly produce 1,000,000 barrels ? Yet such a prediction would have been literally fulfilled. The statements which thus have been made for 330 years of the approaching exhaustion of the herring fishery have, one after another, been falsified by the result. Of course the wolf may come at last. But the shepherd, who has been told for 330 years that the wolf was always coming, and has never yet known him come, may venture to hope for the security of his flock for a little time longer.

But some people are not satisfied with such an argument as this. Their ancestors, they think, may have been wrong in supposing that the limited machinery at their disposal was capable of exhausting the sea. But modern energy has developed the fishery to such an extent that existing appliances for the capture of fish bear no comparison with the old engines which they have superseded. All fish, so they argue, must in one stage of their existence be young and small; if they are killed when they are young, it is impossible that they can grow till they are old; and, by destroying a fish when it is young, we are really killing a creature of no value, which, if we only wait patiently, will become of great value. But, in the first place, people do not act in this way in other matters. They do not hesitate to eat an egg worth a penny, because it might, if it were put into an incubator, be gradually developed into a chicken worth three and sixpence; and in the next place there is no certainty, there is even no reasonable probability that the little fish which a man declined to kill would develop into a mature fish fit for food. On the contrary the chances against it doing so are extraordinarily great. The mortality among fish in the earlier stages of their existence is so large that the destruction of small fish by man, wasteful as it may seem, can have no appreciable effect on the stock of fish in the sea.

To make the foregoing assertion good, it may perhaps be
legitimate to use an illustration, which the present writer
has used twice before, and which has never been answered.
It may be assumed as a matter beyond dispute that
European fishermen are drawing more than 3,000,000,000
of mature herrings annually from the North Sea. It has
been proved that predaceous birds and predaceous fish
catch annually at least as many herrings as are caught by
the fishermen. Yet at the end of the fishing season there
is no perceptible diminution in the size of the shoals. It is
unlikely that one herring out of every thousand has been
killed : it is improbable that one herring out of every
hundred has been killed : it is certain that one herring out
of every ten has not been killed ; but, to put the matter
beyond all doubt, it shall be assumed that one herring out
of every two is killed. In that case 6,000,000,000 herrings
are killed, and 6,000,000,000 herrings are left alive. In
order to maintain the existing stock of herrings in the sea,
these 6,000,000,000 herrings ought, in the course of the
succeeding year, to produce another 6,000,000,000 adult
herrings, or, if half the surviving herrings are females,
each female herring must produce two adult herrings.
But each female herring deposits from 20,000 to 50,000
eggs. Take the lowest of these numbers. Out of every
20,000 eggs which the female herring extrudes, 19,998
herrings must either fail to be hatched, or must perish in
some of the earlier stages of existence. Suppose that man
by his so-called wasteful operations succeeds in destroying
8 out of the 19,998 eggs or fish, or in other words
24,000,000,000 whitebait, nature will still have to account
for the destruction of the remaining 19,990 eggs or young
fish. If she did not do so, the North Sea in the course of
a few years would become a solid mass of herrings.

It is obvious, therefore, that the destruction of fish by man, large as it seems at first sight, is like a drop of water in the bucket when it is compared with the prodigious natural waste which is simultaneously going on. It is absurd, therefore, to suppose that any necessity can exist for restricting the operations of the fishermen. It may perhaps be added that it is almost impossible to devise any regulations which will effectively prevent the capture of immature fish, and which will not simultaneously interfere with the legitimate operations of the fishermen Most, if not all, the modes of fishing involve some waste The most efficient engines of capture are precisely those which are the most destructive ; and any legislative precautions, calculated to preserve the fry of fish, will undoubtedly diminish the supply, and consequently increase the price, of fish as food. People, therefore, who are interested in cheap fish should cease to demand restrictive legislation. The fisheries of the British Islands languished under the patronage of the great, and made no real progress under the patronage of the Legislature. They have attained their present prosperity under a system of freedom. "When the subject enjoys the fruit of his industry," wrote Pope in a note on a well-known passage of the Odyssey, "the earth will always be well cultivated and bring forth abundance ; the sea will furnish the land with plenty of fishes, and men will plant when they are sure to gather the fruit." It was the misfortune of England that her statesmen for one hundred years did not realise the full moral of this passage, or see that the true way to promote every industry was to leave it alone.*

* The passage in Homer is a very remarkable one. "Under a good government," says Ulysses to Penelope, "the land brings forth its fruit, and the sea yields its fish."

These truths require perhaps to be impressed on the public at a moment when one section of the people is endeavouring to impose restrictive regulations on fishermen, and another section is trying, by an unnecessary and therefore unwise patronage, to develop an industry which is already prosperous. But it must not be supposed that, because free trade in fishing is better than protection, and the independence of an honest man is worth more than all the patronage of all the aristocracy, nothing can be done either by legislation or in other ways to promote the development of British fisheries. The few pages to which this essay may still extend, cannot perhaps be more usefully occupied than by considering this portion of the subject.

In the first place, the State can do what no private individual can possibly do. It can collect and publish periodical and authoritative statements of the condition of the fisheries. This information can easily be collected by officers who already exist, and no appreciable expense will therefore be incurred in obtaining it. Its publication will be of great advantage. In State affairs, as in other matters, the possession of knowledge is essential to the administrator ; and many of the wild proposals which are constantly made for the regulation of the fisheries, would probably be dropped if the steady and satisfactory progress of the industry were established by figures. Those who desire to resist the introduction of restrictive laws as well as those who clamour for their passage, are, or ought to be, equally interested in procuring the statistics, by which the soundness of their own opinions must ultimately be tested.

In the next place, the State can provide, or can ask other nations to aid it in providing for what—for want of a better word—may be termed the Police of the Seas. The continuous development of the fishery is constantly making regulations for preserving order and preventing collision more and more necessary. A central authority alone can devise means for regulating the traffic of the ocean, or can determine what lights or other marks shall be borne by distinctive classes of vessels. The State has, from the first, recognized its obligation to discharge this function. But it has still much to do before it can rest from its labours. The whole question of lights at sea—the most important of all the subjects arranged by the State which affects the fisheries—is in a confused and unsatisfactory position. The decision of the Hague Convention is still unratified. These and other questions await solution; and the State, and the State alone, is capable of solving them.

In the third place, though in this respect greater caution is necessary, the State may probably do something to promote the construction of harbours in which the fishing-fleets may find shelter in bad weather, or in which facilities may be afforded for landing fish. The State, indeed, could probably undertake no more pernicious function than the construction of fishing-harbours. If it be once known that the Treasury is willing to build harbours for localities, local bodies and individuals will cease to build them for themselves. The Imperial Exchequer, however liberal it may be, can never hope to do so much as the localities themselves, and its readiness to build harbours will actually lead to fewer harbours being built. The true course, apparently, for the Government, is to encourage local efforts by offering to advance money for the purpose on easy terms. It will thus avoid the embarrassing duty of selecting the precise spots which are most worthy of attention, and it will escape the invidious distinction of preferring one place to another. Much may, indeed, be urged for the policy of constructing one or two harbours of refuge at exposed points of the coast. But such harbours are not required, and ought not to be made for fishing reasons alone; and their provision must be defended on broader grounds than it is possible properly to bring forward in an essay on the fish-trade of the United Kingdom.

These three things—the preparation of adequate statistics; the provision of proper police regulations for ensuring order at sea: and the facilitating the construction of adequate fishing-harbours—are the three points on which the action of the State may properly be employed in promoting the fishing industry. There are one or two minor points in which it is possible that interference may be beneficial, but speaking broadly, on all other matters, State intervention is probably injurious; and the best service that the Government can render to fishermen, is to leave them alone. Mr. Huxley once stated that fishermen should be left to pursue their calling "how they like, when they like, and where they like." As a general proposition, to which Mr. Huxley would probably himself admit a few minor exceptions may be made, the present writer is convinced of the truth of Mr. Huxley's dictum.

Though, however, the action of the State should thus be limited, other persons may do something to promote the fishing-trade. The Corporation of London might assist in this way by improving Billingsgate and its approaches, or by substituting for it some more convenient water-side market. The various railway companies might do something in the same direction by reconsidering the terms on which they now carry fish; while private enterprise might also be of use in devising some adequate scheme for the insurance of fishermen's lives, their boats and their gear. These are means by which both the State and the public may usefully promote the fisherman's industry. Except by such expedients as these, the truest method of assisting fishermen is to leave them alone. The fisherman of the British Islands has attained his present position by his own unaided efforts ; his best friends desire that he should be neither hampered by the restrictions of law nor spoilt by the smiles of patronage. To both dangers he is exposed at the present time. His importance has won for him friends ; and his new friends are always suggesting new legislative regulations for his protection, or for the protection of the fish which he takes. Hitherto these suggestions have been disregarded by Parliament. It may be hoped that the time will never come when they may receive more attention. In fishing, as in other industries, freedom is the first condition of.success, and the man who is fettered by restrictive laws is little better than a slave. Perhaps some readers may recollect what was said of the slave :

> " Jove fixed it certain that whatever day
> Makes man a slave takes half his worth away."

LONDON :

PRINTED BY WILLIAM CLOWES AND SONS, LIMITED,
STAMFORD STREET AND CHARING CROSS.